CUMBRIA LIBRARIES

D0177699

For Whom the Bell Tolls

Light and Dark Verse by
Martin Bell

ICON BOOKS

Published in the UK in 2011 by
Icon Books Ltd, Omnibus Business Centre,
39–41 North Road, London N7 9DP
email: info@iconbooks.co.uk
www.iconbooks.co.uk

Sold in the UK, Europe, South Africa and Asia
by Faber & Faber Ltd, Bloomsbury House,
74–77 Great Russell Street,
London WC1B 3DA or their agents

Distributed in the UK, Europe, South Africa and Asia
by TBS Ltd, TBS Distribution Centre, Colchester Road,
Frating Green, Colchester CO7 7DW

Published in Australia in 2011 by
Allen & Unwin Pty Ltd, PO Box 8500,
83 Alexander Street, Crows Nest, NSW 2065

Distributed in Canada by
Penguin Books Canada,
90 Eglinton Avenue East, Suite 700,
Toronto, Ontario M4P 2YE

ISBN: 978-184831-304-0

Text copyright © 2011 Martin Bell
The author has asserted his moral rights.

No part of this book may be reproduced in any form, or by any
means, without prior permission in writing from the publisher.

Typeset in Minion by Marie Doherty

Printed in Great Britain by
Clays Ltd, St Ives plc

Contents

Foreword

This is as near to an autobiography as I shall write, and I have done it episodically, itinerantly and in verse to reflect the life that I have lived. I tend to feel passionately about things – and that applies as much to the inanities of TV news as to the futilities of warfare; to sleaze and sloths, to celebrities and seagulls and much else. Hence poetry (of a sort) not prose; and the verse is light and dark because the life was.

There is a family history to this. My father, the country writer Adrian Bell, wrote a book of romantic poems early in his life which was kept from us children because they were written to someone other than our mother (and before he met her, as it happened). His father, the journalist Robert Bell, published an ingenious volume of light poetry, *After-thoughts*, in 1929. I have borrowed and included a poem from each as a heartfelt family tribute.

I can hardly claim consistency of output. I wrote the first of these poems, 'Chain of Command', as a soldier on active service in Cyprus in 1958. I did not write another for more than half a century. Then, in December 2009, I was waiting to give evidence about the Bosnian war to the War Crimes Tribunal in The Hague. I was still troubled by the ill-fated decision of the British government to join in the invasion of Iraq in 2003. I fell to wondering why some wars generated criminal processes and others did not. It seemed to depend on who fought them and who won them. So I wrote the flagship poem of this collection, 'Principal Witness', about Tony Blair before the court of history.

Others followed in short order – indeed, they seemed to write themselves – until in a year I found that I had more than a hundred of them. They appeared spontaneously about all sorts of subjects and in all sorts of forms: quatrains, couplets, a sonnet, a ballade, limericks and even a clerihew – plus other forms which so far as I know are not attempted by regular and professional poets, no doubt for the best of reasons.

I am grateful to the many people who have crossed my path and inspired these pieces, friends and others, named or unnamed – including some, like Idi Amin, who are no longer with us.

Most special thanks go to Martin Rowson of *The Guardian* for his cover cartoon. It was originally one of his illustrations for John Sweeney's book about the Tatton adventure, *Purple Homicide – Fear and Loathing on Knutsford Heath*, published by Bloomsbury in 1997. Sweeney described what we were engaged in as not so much an election campaign but rather a pub crawl with attitude. And at one point he came up with the daft idea that I should ride across the constituency on a white horse. Rowson's rumpled Don Quixote derived from that.

The arrangement of these pieces is partly chronological, partly thematic and partly as haphazard as the life that they encompass.

And sometimes, when the rhymes took on a life of their own and galloped away with the memories, I followed them out of curiosity, to see where they might lead. And what is poetry anyway but verse for solemn people?

To the old soldiers of the Suffolk Regiment

London's Burning

One night in Tottenham we crossed a border
Into a land of riot and disorder,
And it's *our* land. We law-abiding Brits
Are now the authors of a home-grown blitz.
We steal, we smash, we torch that bus,
No one's to blame for it but us;
Our sense of who we are is shot to bits,
And wild-eyed tribesmen in Waziristan
Speak sadly of the savage Englishman.

From the dry tinder of a single shooting
Stores are burning, predators are looting;
Across the violent, vicious state we're in
We see the rule of law is wafer-thin:
Our hellfire burns without a fire wall.
The anarchy of mobs and riot-makers
Throws this our capital into free fall;
A nation of shop-keepers? Not at all –
A nation of shop-breakers.

Riotous Illiteracy

*In the rioting that spread across London in August 2011 only
the bookshops were left untouched.*

They looted clothes and trainers, mobile phones,
All goods of glitz and value and utility,
But never even paused at Waterstones,
Seeing its books as objects of futility:

Shakespeare's undrinkable,
Kipling's unthinkable,
Milton's unwearable
Wordsworth's unbearable
(This one at least we'd make allowance for,
The Sage of Lakeland being such a bore).

And as for our inflammatory writers,
Trotsky, Karl Marx and Chomsky – all in vain.
Not even they attracted London's rioters,
Being judged not worth a broken window pane.

So here's the Law of Lawlessness immutable:
Books are declared redundant and unsuitable,
Their words unread, their worth unsung,
Unwanted and unlootable,
By these our feckless and illiterate young.

Murdochracy

The operations of the Digger
Were such that, as his power grew bigger,
The moral jeopardy was graver
For those who sought his *Sun*-lit favour:
To their advantage or to his? Go figure.

Lachlan, Elisabeth and James,
These were the competing names
Of the next generation
Of Murdochisation,
And useful to know:
But again, *Cui bono*?

And those who were willing
To pocket his shilling
Had a name for his fee,
Which they called the Rupee.

The Lesson

Iraq, Afghanistan, now Libya too,
We learned one lesson and we learned it well:
Going to war's the easy thing to do,
But getting out of it is hard as hell.

False Prophet

We followed him, as the half-blinded must;
He was our light – and what the prophet saith,
With eyes ablaze, we tend to take on trust.
We were beguiled. His truths were but a wraith,
His myths of mass destruction turned to dust.
Impenitent, he cut a fateful swathe
From peace to war and then from boom to bust;
And told us falsehoods, always in good faith.
He had this self-belief, and never hid it,
That what he did was right because he did it.
He went for it, pursued the chosen course
And never showed a flicker of remorse.
But in the end the fever in those eyes
Showed something else – and that way madness lies.

The Chilcot Committee

Three mandarins and two professors
Sit around a table:
They are the Iraq War assessors,
So far as they are able.
Let only their *j'accuse* impress us.
It was fought on a fable.

Principal Witness

'Please take a seat, Prime Minister, and stay,
We're interested in what you have to say.'
I only know that what I did was right.
The ghosts of soldiers looked on in dismay.

The written record pulled a rattling coach
And horses through his government's approach.
The case for war was all but watertight.
The ghosts of soldiers looked on in reproach.

The rights and wrongs were neither here nor there;
Admire the spin, the twist, the fine veneer.
Of course I can sleep easily at night.
The ghosts of soldiers looked on in despair.

The shock and awe were easy to assess,
One called it 'a catastrophic success'.
For Basra and Baghdad the future's bright.
The ghosts of soldiers looked on in distress.

Others had testified that, in their eyes,
The post-war plan was chaos in disguise.
I knew it would be all right on the night.
The ghosts of soldiers looked on in surprise.

Pay tribute to the fallen, share the grief,
Ah, that's the way to do it, brave and brief.
For all we stood to gain, the costs were light.
The soldiers' ghosts looked on in disbelief.

Forty Years On

At school he didn't join the CCF
(Army cadets), he said he wouldn't play
Toy soldiers, and he therefore stayed away.
He was indifferent to the point of deaf
To bugle calls and trumpets from afar;
He much preferred the sounds of his guitar.

Forty years on, as head of government,
He loved to walk along the mustered ranks,
And radiate among the troops and tanks;
His attitude to war was different,
And for a while it helped his fortunes thrive;
The troops, however, did not all survive.

In Memoriam

If you should wonder why we breathed our last,
It was because of his sincere convictions,
The flotsam tide of falsehoods floating past,
The fantasies to which he clung so fast.
The false prospectus hammered to the mast,
The narrative as flaw-flecked as the cast,
And certainties that turned out to be fictions.

The Journey

In the tradition of the music hall
And those who trod its boards, Eric and Ernie,
Are those TV producers, comics all,
Whose opening gambit is always the same,
Before we've even shot a single frame;
They say to me, 'Just take us on a journey'.

Our late Prime Minister, so messianic
His ship of state became the new *Titanic*,
Was always journeying. The route he took,
Inspiring everything from awe to panic,
Was from one war zone to the next, and look,
It then became the title of his book.

Through Kosovo, Baghdad and Kandahar,
His journeys weren't at all run of the mill,
But lured him into battlefields too far;
And we were with him for a while, until
We saw the merit of just standing still
And journeying no further than the bar.

Chain of Command

The view from the ranks of the 1st Battalion the Suffolk Regiment: lines written in Cyprus in 1958 for the regimental magazine Castle and Key. *I also did the accounts for the Corporals' Mess.*

The Major General cut himself while shaving,
And cursed the Brigadier who, madly raving,
Then cast the most chastising and infernal
Aspersions on the morals of the Colonel;
Who passed them to the Major, and he, rapt in
The darkest thoughts, relayed them to the Captain,
Who rocketed the Subaltern who rose
To loose all hell among the NCOs,
Who in their wrath and mad acerbity
Picked on one last poor buckshee Private – me!

Bash on Regardless

In 1957 when I was a young soldier before the War Office Selection Board, the presiding Brigadier concluded that I was not officer material and returned me to regimental duty. Bash on Regardless *was the motto of the old Army Commandos.*

The first of life's inspections that I failed
Was the Army's officer selection test.
The smarter, brighter, smoother ones prevailed;
I was of course the awkwardest
In any awkward squad. The Brigadier
Told Private Bell to take himself elsewhere.

Bless him, for those two years in the ranks
Taught more than any university.
The officer's entitlements? No thanks,
Besides, they were as thick as two short planks,
Not to be entrusted with a troop of tanks.
Better the uses of adversity:
That was the lesson of the Corporals' Mess;
We learn much more from failure than success.

The golden hopefuls of my generation,
The future bishops, ministers of state
And such, were victims of high expectation,
But crashed and burned on take-off, every one,
Defrocked or brought before the magistrate
In circumstances that intrigued *The Sun*.

But we, who were the RSM's despair,
We slowly and discreetly raised our game,
We learned sufficient arms drill on the square,
Did not disgrace the regimental name,
And by not being spectacularly good,
We went much further than he thought we would.

So here's the moral of this soldier's story:
Don't ever dream of trailing clouds of glory;
Play the long game, don't try to fly too high
And never catch the Sergeant Major's eye.
Life's not a sprint but more a marathon;
The winner is the one who bashes on.

Call Signs

*From 1957 to 1959 I was a soldier in the Intelligence Section of
the Suffolk Regiment in Cyprus.*

When I served in the ranks the then CO
Was known as Sunray on the radio,
Which we who knew him thought inapposite,
Since he was not conspicuously bright.
The Signals Officer was code-named Seagull,
To which he was in literacy the equal.
Lest our identities should be mistaken,
We in Intelligence were known as Acorn;
My military career was never finer
Than when I used the call sign Acorn Minor.
Yet from this acorn grew no mighty oak
But just a wandering and insurgent bloke.

Look East

*I began my broadcasting career with the BBC in Norwich in
1962. The news programme we launched two years later was
rather less slick and professional than the* Look East *of today.*

One day in autumn 1964,
Quite unremarked in television's folklore,
The BBC began the worst and least
Distinguished programme in its history,
Less of a broadcast than a travesty
And parody of regular TV
(A sort of Alan Partridge show,
But from so very long ago).
The hapless debutant was called *Look East*:
And Old East Anglians remember well
Their daily diet of television from hell
Inflicted by a youthful Martin Bell.

Nigeria

The United Kingdom supported the Nigerian government in its war against the secessionists of Biafra, formerly Eastern Nigeria, from 1967 to 1969. The government forces won.

We sold them armaments and armoured cars,
Equipped their rag-tag army with the best,
Staff College trained their generals (two stars),
And well-placed mercenaries did the rest;
Then when their war machine was deadliest,
We piously denied that it was ours.

We leased them aircraft about which we lied,
Jet trainers, pilots, bombardiers and more.
(They dropped their bombs from DC3s, port side).
We fuelled a fire we never answered for,
And here I learned a principle of war:
There is no truth until it is denied.

Armagh

In the late 1960s in Northern Ireland I was not one of The Reverend Ian Paisley's favourite reporters, although inadvertently I helped to bring him to national attention. Thirty years later, when we served in the House of Commons together, he could not have been more affable.

The Big Man called his people to the square,
Not for a rally but a day of prayer.
They sought deliverance from all their foes:
I was identified as one of those.
He said I didn't serve the BBC,
But the dark forces of the Papacy.
He urged his people not to harm a hair
And added, 'But he's standing over there!'
The Big Man's motto of 'No popery'
Seemed in my case to be more like 'No hopery'.
Surrounded and with no way of retreating,
His loyal people gave me quite a beating.

Idi Amin

President Idi Amin of Uganda married his fifth wife, Sarah,
at the OAU Summit in Kampala in 1975.

In fifty years I never played the hero
And never was one either, more's the pity;
In derring-do my rating was a zero –
I did not lead an infantry attack,
I never claimed to liberate a city,
Or counted them all out and then all back.

But one thing that I did and they did not,
Despite their valiant actions and embeddings
(Except of course that some of us were shot),
The sole, unique distinction I have got:
I witnessed one of Idi Amin's weddings,
To Lady Sarah of the Suicide Squad
Of the Ugandan Army; and that, by God,
Was well worth doing, if distinctly odd.

St Lucia

The island of St Lucia, once a British possession, became an independent state on 22 February 1979.

The flags were lowered, one by one,
In the direction of the setting sun,
On islands soon to be ex-colonies;
A free St Lucia would be one of these.

It seemed ill-starred: a frigate rammed the quays
Of the island's port and capital, Castries;
A petrol strike made public transport fail;
The prisoners rioted and burned the jail.
Perhaps imprudently, I felt I ought
Include these mishaps in the day's report.
The island's very displeased government
Imposed a Caribbean punishment.
(The option of imprisonment was void,
Because the prison cells had been destroyed.)
A favoured band, the True Tones, wrote a song
Accusing me of every kind of wrong.
They sang: 'Martin Bell of the BBC,
He's the man we really want to see.
The BBC should be ashamed
To associate itself with Martin Bell's name.'

A calypso's editorial in those parts,
And this one even topped the island's charts.
Hoping that all's forgotten over time,
Except of course the rhythm and the rhyme,
I seek no glittering prizes, because *ipso
Facto*, I have got my own calypso.

The Cavalry

In Gulf War One in 1991 I was embedded with a British tank regiment, The Queen's Royal Irish Hussars, commanded by Lieutenant Colonel Arthur Denaro.

To say they didn't like to leave their horses
Is understatement. Given half a chance,
Even now they'd willingly set sail for France,
To fight old battles with equestrian forces.

The cornets (subalterns) have to pretend
Their polo pony is their closest friend
Or else be Duty Officer for weeks on end.

Traditions stick: a new recruit called Trevor
Was told it wasn't on their list of names.
The Colonel ordered: 'Henceforth and for ever
The Regiment is going to call you James!'

Dismounted, they won't march the extra mile,
Or any miles at all, it's not their style,
But they make up for it with charm and guile.

With some reluctance they retrained on tanks
And learned reconnaissance in armoured cars;
How they survived at all remains a mystery;
But still, some fine old titles left their ranks:
My favourite among these last hurrahs
For sure, The Queen's Royal Irish Hussars,
A rather splendid fighting force
Well known to some as Arthur's Horse;
Also: the Queerest Regiment in History.

A Political Romance

I was the BBC's Chief North America Correspondent during the eight years of the special relationship between Ronald Reagan and Margaret Thatcher. No other visiting head of government was received at the White House with such attention and affection.

It had the aspect of a high romance,
Such as no novelist could represent,
A minuet, or diplomatic dance
Between Prime Minister and President.

This was no routine meeting on his list,
He the great illusionist
And she the handbag specialist,
Being not so much a summit as a tryst.

They seemed so much at one in their rapport
(Glances exchanged and confidences heeded)
That it was said she told him what she thought
And told him then what *he* did.

Vukovar

This fine old Austro-Hungarian town on the banks of the Danube was totally destroyed by artillery and tank fire during the Croatian war in November 1991. The Chetniks, roaming bands of Serbian irregulars, were the ground troops who forced the Croats' surrender at the end of a long siege.

A Balkan Stalingrad – as Serbian tanks
Blasted the cemetery, and Chetniks fought
From house to house along the river banks;
The centre shook and fell, the suburbs bled;
I stood among the ruins and I thought,
It isn't even safe here to be dead.

From the destructions of the war machine
In all the zones of conflict where I've been
(At the last reckoning there were eighteen),
Plus other random bloodshed in between,
I'd say to those who glamorise
The warrior's toil and trouble,
That 'To the victor goes the prize,
Which is a pile of rubble'.*

---

* *A quotation from one of my reports from Vukovar in November 1991.*

Lucky Escape

In June 1992 the runway of Sarajevo airport was a free fire zone, with government forces on both its sides and the Serbs at its ends; but it was the only way into the city. The BBC car was a battered Vauxhall Carlton.

I drove at speed across the airport runway,
And, half way over, hit a spot of bother,
Or it hit me. As I was going one way
A burst of hostile fire came from another.

Yet I got through unscathed. The bullets sank
Into the door frame without passing through it.
My friends at Vauxhall Cars had made a tank,
And in the fog of war they never knew it.

Holiday Inn Sarajevo

It was the ultimate war zone hotel,
Its south side blown away by shot and shell,
Apparently the lodging place from hell
And yet, away from where the mortars fell,
It did not just survive, but cast its spell;
It was our refuge and it served us well.

The Serbian snipers had it in their sights,
The comforts of a hostelry were few,
No running water, little food, no lights
And rather short on health and safety too.

Of course it never quite ran out of booze,
In those days the chief lubricant of news,
And made up for a scarcity of wines
With its supply of bootleg Ballantines.

To those who ran away it seemed accursed,
More like ground zero than a place of rest.
By normal standards it was quite the worst,
But to us war zone folk it seemed the best,
We the believers, they the infidels,
In this most dangerous of all hotels,
And those who stayed there were uniquely blessed.

Vitez

*This central Bosnian town was the base for British peacekeeping
troops throughout the Bosnian war from 1992 to 1995.*

We came upon it in the midst of war,
Muslims and Croats, not a Serb in sight;
We should have seen it as a metaphor:
Its only factory made dynamite.
Here in the school the British troops were based,
Without a mandate, peacekeeping *ad hoc*,
As all around them murderers laid waste,
And every one would own his own road block.

And so amid the Balkan cauldron's pressures
The best of British learned to improvise.
First up, the 22nd of Foot, the Cheshires,
(The Guards of course did their own thing, Guards-wise),
'Flowers of the Forest' – the Scots too knew the cost.
It was a long haul and hard earned success,
Lives saved which otherwise would have been lost,
And every man owned his own peace process.

Twenty years on and what a transformation!
No footfall of the bloodshed and hardship;
The place became a racketeers' way station,
A Balkan Vegas or suburban strip,
With nightclubs and casinos wall to wall;
Some lost their lives and others prospered well,
There was no decent outcome there at all,
And every man would own his private hell.

Karadzic on Trial

Dr Karadzic was arrested in Belgrade in June 2009 after more than ten years on the run. (He called it his 'period of avoidance'.) He conducted his own defence at his trial at The Hague which began in March 2010. I appeared as a prosecution witness in December 2010. He asked me to visit him before the court appearance.

He sat before me in a guarded cell,
And though I once believed I knew him well,
It seemed our altered lives ran parallel,
As if in separate ante-rooms of hell.

He vowed he'd left his heart and his possessions
Inside a city of beloved sadness;
And yet I knew, because of his obsessions,
His soldiers bombed it to the edge of madness.

The siege of Sarajevo was refought,
No longer street by street and trench by trench,
But mercilessly and in open court,
On screens inset into the judges' bench.

He called me precious: 'precious witness'. *What!*
No one in all my troubled life and times
Had ever spoken of me thus – and that
Was from a man indicted for war crimes.

For all the sacrifices of the dead,
The legend of the cause of those he led
Will ricochet for ever in the head
Of one who talked of maps while others bled.

Ratko Mladic

General Ratko Mladic, former commander of the Bosnian Serb Army, was indicted by the War Crimes Tribunal in 1996. He was arrested in Northern Serbia on 26 May 2011 and extradited to The Hague to face trial on charges relating to the siege of Sarajevo and the Srebrenica massacre.

We knew his scowl, his cold contempt, his swagger,
This Balkan incarnation of Macbeth;
A trail of bloodshed stained the path he trod
From Srebrenica to Bosanski Brod.
He too was brave and he too dealt in death.
He had a soldier's hand upon the dagger,
Or in this case the execution squad,
For which he now must answer before God,
As God in mercy or in wrath disposeth,
And to the Court, until his dying breath.

The Court observes the processes of law,
Consideration of the rules of war
And all protections due to the accused;
Such rights as were notoriously refused
To victims of his deadliest attack:
All they got was a bullet in the back.

Arkan

*The Serbian warlord Zeljko Raznatovic, also known as Arkan,
was assassinated in Belgrade on 15 December 2000. Most
Croats are Roman Catholics. During the Croatian war the Serbs
dismantled their churches in both Petrinja and Erdut, which was
Arkan's headquarters.*

Here was a man who lived not by the sword
But rather by the gun and hand grenade;
He was a lethal gangster and warlord
Who owned an ice cream parlour in Belgrade.

I knew him well: and over the ice cream
He would outline his people's destiny,
Their history, their legend and their dream,
One nation from the Danube to the sea.

He hated Croats and he hated Turks
(His word for Muslims), and he drew up lists
Of Tito's followers and all their works,
For most of all he hated Communists.

By *force majeure* he managed to recruit
An army called the Tigers, widely feared,
Based in the Croatian village of Erdut,
From which the church mysteriously disappeared.

He seized a mascot from the Belgrade Zoo,
A tiger cub his soldiers idolised;
The beast proved hard to handle – his men too,
Who pillaged, looted, killed and terrorised

Through two republics, Bosnia and Croatia;
Their war of conquest knew no boundaries,
It seemed they specialised in the erasure
Not just of lives but of identities.

Under his real name of Raznatovic
He was of course indicted by the Court,
But died before the lawyers worked out which
Of many war crimes charges should be brought.

His end, alas, was very far from gentle,
Unloved, unmourned, uncherished and unlit,
Gunned down inside the Intercontinental:
Who lives by the grenade will die by it.

White Suits

They had no meaning ethical or moral
But helped to keep me safe; while on a mission
To tell the story of some distant quarrel
I comforted myself with superstition.

So in the Balkans twenty years ago
The snipers and the gunners aimed and missed.
I was a winter warfare specialist,
And much the best protected journalist:
The suits were also camouflage in snow.

War Plugs

The danger level was high and rising higher,
We dealt with mortars, snipers, gangs of thugs;
What vexed me most was not incoming fire
But the near total absence of bath plugs.

Washbasins, baths and sinks – it seemed symbolic
Of a society in disarray:
Wherever we would go some plugaholic
Had nicked the plugs and taken them away.

I solved the problem rather well, I think;
I hit upon a plug (one size fits all)
That could adapt to any war zone sink.
My prized possession was a soft squash ball.

Wildlife

The Sloth

One day beneath a tree in Costa Rica
I had my special moment of Eureka.
I saw a creature upside down therein,
And thought, this could be either or be both:
The sloth is named for the deadly sin,
Or the deadly sin for the sloth.

The Egret

It is to me a cause of deepest regret
That we, unlike the nimble-footed egret,
Should plod the earth with mortal tread
Heavy enough to wake the dead;
I only wish we knew the egret's secret.

The Seagull

Since seagulls are so common everywhere,
You might think of them as a band of brothers,
But there's a pecking order in the air:
It seems that some are more seagull than others.

Bird's Nest

The cat looked up at the bird in its nest,
The bird looked down at the cat:
Somewhere we must have sinned and erred,
For ours is the plight and the perch of the bird,
And we too face the deadliest
Of threats to life and habitat,
And the fate, like the bird's, of coming off second best.
We are beset by tooth and claw,
Too well aware of what they're for
And who they're aiming at.

The Canaries

These are not birds but footballers. I have been a lifelong
supporter of Norwich City. Its saviour and majority shareholder
Delia Smith began her TV career, as I did, with the BBC
in Norwich. In 2011 the Canaries won promotion from the
Championship and returned to their rightful place in the
Premier League.

The nerves of Norwich fans could not be steelier;
They've had to be, through every up and down,
Especially a clash with Ipswich Town.
Just once we had a mighty brush with fame,
When we returned triumphant from Bavaria;
But mostly, missing sitters in the area,
We struggled in mid-table. Yet through Delia
(OK, you waited for that rhyme
But got it – didn't you? – in time)
We have the best cuisine in all the game;
And like one of her soufflés, newly risen,
We're now back in the Premier Division.

Such is her hold on all of our supporters,
That they remained obedient to her orders
When she explored a well-remembered avenue
With the immortal war cry 'Let's be 'aving you!'

Giuseppe Verdi

He wrote his operas to great acclaim,
Grand marches, overtures, *La Traviata*,
But still I wonder what lies in a name:
Would his successes have been quite the same,
And he so sovereign on the music scene,
If Bermondsey had been his *alma mater*,
And he'd been one of us, just plain Joe Green?

Ode to Marmite

'I don't think that I'll ever write a poem as lovely as Marmite'
Advertisement on a jar of Marmite

Dark and pungent, dense and glutinous,
Either we love you dearly or are mutinous.
While some of us will swear allegiance
To your mysterious ingredients,
Others will nervously recoil
From your resemblance to slick-oil,
And foreigners so little understand you,
The dreadful Danes have actually banned you!

But lovelier than a poem? There I think
You push comparatives a bit too far.
And yet you save us from the demon drink,
And the intoxications of a bar,
When we decide to have another jar.

On Entering Parliament

My four years as an MP, from 1997 to 2001, were the most disappointing and even shocking of my life, in terms of the discrepancy between what I hoped for in the House of Commons and what I found there.

When first I walked in past the grand statues,
I thought, now here's a lesson I can use
About the values of democracy;
This is its beating heart and pantheon.
But then I went to my first PMQs
And wondered, what's this feeble, lame excuse
For firing endless volleys of abuse,
What is this waste of space, this travesty?
And such a shameful way to carry on;
If that's the best that Parliament can do,
I should have bought a ticket to the zoo.

The Backbencher

No need to whip the poor backbencher
With threats of punishment or censure,
For seeing what the man will do
Unwhipped, there is no reason to.

Requiem

Indifferent to the people's warning,
The parties headed for a fall,
Tory, Labour and Lib Dem.
At the going down of the sun and in the morning,
We will of course remember them,
But miss them not at all.

Bought and Sold

*One day in the House of Commons I saw a well-respected MP,
on an issue where he could influence others, vote against his
conscience and in support of his party. He was rewarded with
a peerage.*

He seemed a decent sort, upright and staid,
And frugal too: no duck house and no moat,
By no means an expenses renegade,
His reputation was his stock in trade,
And yet I swear I saw him sell his vote.

In a division where he carried weight
He was the Whips' appointed candidate
To lead the way with deeds rather than words.
And so he voted to capitulate
And now he sits in ermine in the Lords.

Sleaze Then and Now

It almost seemed an age of innocence
Back then: the merest handful of MPs,
Some of them charlatans and others fools,
Took cash for questions, cheated, cooked the books,
And when these peccadilloes became known,
They were not much more than a public joke.

But now the Members thrive at our expense,
Surfing a tide of larceny and sleaze,
Acting of course within their precious rules;
We also know that half of them are crooks.
The scandal is entirely home-grown;
Our whole democracy's gone up in smoke.

This is a time for public penitence:
They will no longer pilfer as they please.
The ballot box contains our real crown jewels.
We shall prevail – it's harder than it looks,
Until we understand we're not alone,
And we can fix the system that they broke.

Swindlers' List

I wish I had my own duck house,
Redacted and anonymous,
A shaded pool where ducks could float,
A pond, a river or a moat,
A place unto the manor born
Where moles would not uproot the lawn.
I was not born to privilege,
But loitered at the water's edge
And played the Honourable Member
From January to December.
I wish to thank the voters' sense
For choosing me at their expense;
On their behalf I did my best,
Including things they never guessed.
Though my accomplishments were zero,
In fiddling I was next to Nero;
I was a self-philanthropist,
Master of the John Lewis list;
I had a profitable innings
And duly pocketed the winnings,
The subsidies, the perks, the pay,
The petty cash, the ACA,
The Tudor beams, the chandeliers,
The bills for swimming pool repairs,
The hanging plants, the trouser press;
Nothing exceeded like excess:
The whirlpool bath, the horse manure,
Whiter than white, purer than pure.
And so it was until, alas,

The MPs' scandals came to pass.
I was your Honourable Friend,
A pity that it had to end.
And then to avoid the sneers of Mr Paxman
I wrote a cheque and sent it to the taxman.

Sonnet: The People's Bell Tower

In discharge of their parliamentary duties,
And incidentally the pursuit of power,
Our MPs perpetrated some real beauties.
The hanging baskets, duck house and bell tower:
Wodehouse, you should be living at this hour
(Did Blandings Castle also have a moat?).
Forgive the idiom, but *what a shower!*
And all elected on the people's vote.

They may have done some service now and then,
But took us for a ride and robbed us rotten;
Surely we shall not be deceived again,
Nor will their misdemeanours be forgotten.
Henceforth let no man ever have the nerve
To say we get the Members we deserve.

Regrets

Being an Honourable Member for four years,
I mourn the opportunities I lost
To install stable lights and chandeliers,
And tennis courts, complete with their repairs,
To lay a Wilton carpet on the stairs,
To add some Louis Quatorze dining chairs,
Accountants' fees for trading stocks and shares,
And wreaths for the Remembrance Sunday prayers,
Plus free pork pies and crisps and chocolate squares,
To pay all mortgages, debts and arrears,
Not at my own, but someone else's cost.

Instead of representing people's wills,
I could have built up an impressive stash,
Hundreds a month in supermarket bills
And generous amounts of petty cash.

My great regret, if anyone should ask it,
The most conspicuous error that I made,
Was buying a millennium hanging basket:
Its colours were of every hue and shade,
Red, blue and yellow were all in the mix,
A symbol, or a sort of visual aid
For new and more harmonious politics.
It then adorned my house for all that summer.
How could I know the taxpayer would have paid
For that, as for the mole traps of John Gummer?

Behind Bars

David Chaytor, former Labour MP for Bury North, was convicted of fraud and imprisoned in January 2011. Three other ex-MPs, Eric Illsley, Jim Devine and Elliot Morley, followed him.

And so at last the prison door
Slams shut behind an ex-MP
Of dubious reputation.
We have to ask how many more
Who used to keep his company
Deserve his destination.

Brief Encounter

Somewhere remote and safe, out in the sticks,
Amid a photo op of troops and tanks,
A politician walked along the ranks,
Expressing his condolences and thanks.
A soldier threw some words into the mix:
'Sir, how much do you know of soldiering?'
'Not much,' he said, 'in fact, hardly a thing,
But how much do you know of politics?'
'Not much again' – he looked him in the eyes:
'Except, I'm rather good at telling lies.'

Limerick (1): WMD

There once was a great fantasist
Who published a dossier or list
Of a whole armoury
Of WMD,
Which were weapons that didn't exist.

Limerick (2): IDS

Ian Duncan Smith
Seems not to have asked himself if
When the war party beckoned,
Led by George Bush the Second,
He was shafting his own kin and kith.

Clerihew

Prime Minister Anthony Lynton Blair
By messianic zeal and force of will
Marched the Queen's soldiers up the hill
And then he left them there.

Due Process

The soldier, being asked to draw his sword,
Might well have left it sheathed and wondered why;
The war was difficult to justify,
The pretext was entangled in a lie,
The costs were not so hard to prophesy:
At home, the coffins carried shoulder high,
The massed uncounted casualties abroad.
The growing public clamour and discord,
The deep misgivings of the Army Board,
The doubts of diplomats were all ignored.

The lawyerly advice was disregarded
(So, what on earth were all those lawyers for?),
Due processes were bypassed and discarded,
Because of the temptations of a war
To one who would so easily succumb
To the seductions of a distant drum.

Forty Five Minutes

The claim was clear, without a caveat,
No doubt or reservation left within it;
That the dictator's arsenal could threaten,
And his assembled weaponry strike at
Our soil within a mere forty-five-minute
Time span – only a blink to Armageddon.

The claim was false. There's still a mystery why it
Should ever have passed through the sifters' screen
As usable real world intelligence.
Jack Straw admitted they'd been haunted by it,
And so by God they surely should have been,
Considering those who died in consequence.

We wonder what on earth these people think,
Enclosed within their parliamentary bubble,
Who forfeit lives while hardly drawing breath;
They'll take a peaceful nation to the brink,
Turn villages in target zones to rubble,
And sentence unknown innocents to death.

Political Gymnastics

The practice of politicians that gives us the most bother
Is that of saying one thing and then doing another.
Nothing new there of course:
Cromwell said they had no more religion than his horse.
An MP who believes that the earth goes round the sun
and that is that
Will cheerfully vote for a government motion that the
earth is flat.
With only a despatch box as the prize,
He'll back a war based on a pack of lies.
Consider the Right Honourable Jack Straw,
Then Foreign Secretary (or Minister for War),
Whose doubts about Iraq were quite emphatic,
But whose twists and turns were downright acrobatic.
He wrote privately that the case was far from clear,
And then publicly defended it at the UN and elsewhere.
If they disappoint
To that extent
And don't repent,
Then what's the bloody point?

Minister of State

He made his reputation in committee;
His special skill was to negotiate
Conflicts of interest within the City,
And now he is a Minister of State.
Suited and suave, he's ignorant of the pity
Of war, and yet the power to annihilate
Lies with the Honourable Walter Mitty.
And his decisions seal a soldier's fate.

Retreat from Basra

*General Lord Dannatt, Chief of the General Staff from 2006 to
2009, is now Constable of the Tower of London.*

He was installed Chief of the General Staff
When truths about the war were still unspoken,
The costs and casualties were off the graph,
His cherished Army close to being broken.

We had of course fought in Iraq before,
Emblazoned on so many battle honours;
But had as often lost as won the war;
Lessons of history rested lightly on us.

His doubts and reservations were not shared
By politicians who denied defeat.
And so he risked his future and declared
The time had come for orderly retreat.

A deal was duly struck with hostile forces,
His soldiers pulled out at the dead of night,
Lacking the will, the strength and the resources;
It was no victory, more a *Dunkirk lite*.

Through all our history it's been the fate
Of those who ventured to speak truth to power:
For challenging the wisdom of the state,
The state would then consign them to the Tower.

They did not hang him at the Traitor's Gate,
But still he felt the ministers' displeasure;
The Constable did not capitulate.
Crown jewels are not the Tower's only treasure.

Hearts and Minds

The operation's winning minds and hearts,
Or so we're told, until the shooting starts;
And then the hovering Apaches smother
The Taliban (or not) with cannon fire
And bombs and shells and missiles of all kinds,
Under the euphemism of air cover.
Collateral damage, once it was called 'spillage',
Disintegrates another Afghan village.
The casualties, both theirs and ours, rise higher;
And all it's ever doing for hearts and minds
Is blowing them apart from one another.

Wootton Bassett

The flag-draped coffins now exceed twelve score
And counting, for the news grows ever worse.
The town's become a funeral corridor;
A tearful child throws flowers on a hearse.

These last homecomings are a metaphor
For feelings we can't otherwise express:
Condolences from Regiment and Corps
Carry no comfort for the fatherless.

And these are just the casualties we know;
Others are shadows lurking in the past,
The bruisings of the mind take years to show,
But come to haunt their victims at the last.

The overarching question: what's it for?
We cannot take leave of our history,
We know we've fought these Afghan wars before:
This is our fourth, who won the other three?

And back at base, the men whose war this is,
Men without medals, worry more and more:
'These obsequies place too much emphasis
Upon the costs and casualties of war.'

To which we say: 'Look well on scenes like this,
The outcomes of your orders. Show the gains
To set against this tide of casualties;
And when have we prevailed on Afghan plains?'

The Rifleman

Felled by a roadside bomb he never saw,
He lost both of his legs in 'Panther's Claw',
Another victim of our longest war;
And with its scale of casualties revealed
He has the right to ask what it was for.
Or are we British going to do once more
What we have done so many times before,
Declare a victory and leave the field?

Prisoners of War

*The 18th (East Anglian) Division landed in Singapore a few
days before its surrender to the Japanese in February 1942.
The division included three battalions of the Royal Norfolk
Regiment and two battalions of the Suffolk Regiment. They are
remembered each year, on the third Sunday in May, at a service
in the Church of Our Lady and St Thomas of Canterbury in
Wymondham, Norfolk.*

The doomed 18th Division went to war
To serve in undefended Singapore;
And there, inside the fallen citadel,
It suffered the captivity from hell.

All but a handful have departed from us
And each year, at Our Lady and St Thomas,
We honour those who paid the final price,
And wonder at their needless sacrifice.

So to today – and is it not the essence
Of folly that once more our battle groups,
The best and bravest of our fighting troops,
Are sent on far-flung, futile expeditions?
The lesson of the history of these missions
Is still the same: we do not learn its lessons.

Loitering Munitions

Americans don't leave their foes to wonder,
Their words of war both threaten and inform.
An operation codenamed Rolling Thunder
Will do just what it says, like Desert Storm.

By contrast, ours are cryptic as they can be:
Afghanistan is Operation Herrick,
Gulf War One, mysteriously, was Granby,
Its bastard progeny was branded Telic.

But that's the way with war. We are unwilling
To look it in the face and contemplate
The bloody thing it is, a way of killing
That's organised and licensed by the state.

In warfare words like weapons can be fissile;
A bomb is a 'precision guided missile'.
The battlefield is filtered through a prism
Of weasel words and subtle euphemism.

The sacrifice of innocent life and limb
Requires a sort of verbal pirouette:
'Collateral damage' that we did to him
Comes gift-wrapped with the spokesman's 'deep regret'.

The human separations of a blitz
Are outcomes that we find it hard to face;
Blowing a crowded market place to bits
Is merely 'the control of battle space'.

Pilotless aircraft, drones and UAVs
Patrol the skies on surreptitious missions,
Dispensing hell and havoc as they please
Through laser-guided 'loitering munitions'.

'If you could see what we have seen of war ...'
That was the theme of Owen and Sassoon.
Alas, there's no such witness any more,
Only a Reid, an Ainsworth or a Hoon.

Foreboding

Lines written in the Hiroshima Peace Park

We can't afford a future like our past,
And, short of a redemption at the last,
Our fall-out is so clearly one another's,
We need at least a better set of rules.
The choice before us is to live like brothers
Or else to die like fools.

The Nuclear Option

Consider the advances we have made,
The science and technology of ours,
The symphony, the waltz, the serenade,
The arch, the dome, the spire, the colonnade;
The benefits of industry and trade.
We land men on the moon, reach for the stars,
We photograph the surfaces of Mars.

And yet ... we deal in death in arms bazaars,
We make a killing selling armoured cars;
And with the Trident due for an upgrade
The nuclear Frankenstein makes us afraid.
And thus what threatens us in perpetuity
Is just our own accursed ingenuity.

It seems the Devil is a scientist
And we, his most conniving of assistants,
Through the equations of the physicist
Can blow to kingdom come our whole existence.

Our creativity's of little worth
If we unleash it to afflict the Earth
And other forms of life by land and sea
In every way less dangerous than we.

Appeasement

Children of Munich – I am one of them,
Born in ill-favoured 1938 –
Are short on heroism. Our ideal state
Is not a shining city on a hill,
Nor do we seek a New Jerusalem.
We notice what the Triumph of the Will
Achieved in Basra, Baghdad and Erbil.
And over time we've had more than our fill
Of those whose life's ambition is to kill:
Enough of fighting – let's negotiate.

Moonshine

'I am sick and tired of fighting – its glory is all moonshine'
General William Tecumseh Sherman, 1865

Their dreams of war, straight from the silver screen,
Are of John Wayne, George Scott and David Niven;
They'll take that trench and storm that hill. Dream-driven,
The war games of the young can be forgiven.
The truth of it is something yet unseen.
They view the clash of men and arms as thrilling
And, training for it, will be more than willing
To play their part in state-mandated killing.

The war they find is quite another story;
Counting the costs of it, wounded and dead,
Merely a waste of time and lives – its glory
Is all moonshine, as General Sherman said.

The fantasies of heroism subside,
The bugle calls and muffled drumbeats cease;
And those who soldiered on the darker side
Are the most powerful advocates of peace.

Libya

The Typhoons and Tornados overhead
Will spike his guns and waste his arsenals.
By taking out the tank and howitzer
They'll turn the tide and stem the casualties.
Beneath the No Fly Zone (the NFZ)
His four decades of tyranny lie dead,
The people win and the dictator falls –

Except the story is a pack of lies.
Recall the massacre at Srebrenica:
It too happened under guarded skies.
Airpower, the military Wizard of Oz,
Was not decisive then and never was.
No better strategy was ever found
Than bashing on with boots upon the ground.

History

'What lessons should I learn if my ambition
Is first and foremost just to stay alive?'
The young man asked. The old man answered thus:
'All other studies are superfluous,
Where nothing counts but *landmine recognition*.
If you don't know it, you will not survive.'

The young man said: 'Then please address this mystery:
In countries where the wars do not contrive
To plant their devils' gardens on the land,
What does it serve us best to understand?'
'*History*,' he said, '*just history and more history*.
Neglect that too and you will not survive.'

Medal Parade

The Generals of my youth were bright and zestful,
Loyal, ambitious and extremely keen;
But times were peaceful and they lacked a chest full
Of medals given by a grateful Queen.

The GSMs of course came with the ration,
Like OBEs to which they all aspired,
But gongs for gallantry were not in fashion.
They turned to the right, saluted and retired.

Much like the case of Captain Mainwaring
Who had to cancel a full dress parade,
Since medal-wise he didn't have a thing,
So Corporal Jones would put him in the shade.

It's different now. With politicians partial
To putting on a military show,
We've Sergeants with more gongs than a Field Marshal,
And Corporals starting on their second row.

And surely one must not be jealous, must one,
To see the soldiers standing proud and tall?
But knowing that the cause of war's a just one
Would be the grandest trophy of them all.

The Lighthouse

*This seafaring legend derives from a series of radio messages said
to have been exchanged between the Americans and Canadians
in the north Atlantic in 1994.*

The Americans, sensing trouble up ahead,
Confronted the Canadians and said
They risked a course collision and should head
Twelve degrees north, or else be targeted.

The Canadians responded, 'Zut alors!'
(For they were Québecois) – 'No one can force
Us proud Canadians to change our course;
We strongly recommend that you change yours.'

The Americans, with mounting wrath and ire,
Then upped the ante several notches higher,
And ordered the Canadians to retire,
Or the whole battle group would open fire.

Came the reply, 'We're not a ship at all,
But just a lighthouse on a rock – your call.'

A Study in Contrasts

The Honourable Humphrey Ponsonby MP,
Now serving his fifth term, is not without
A sense of his importance to the nation.
His luxury's a new plasma TV;
An emergency's a falling out
With his constituency association;
A fallen comrade is a party friend
Whose term has come to a disgraceful end.

Private Tom Atkins of the Fusiliers
By contrast, under rifle fire and mortar,
Is in his second war zone in three years.
His luxury – a bucket of clean water;
Emergency – a Taliban attack
Involving IEDs and casual slaughter;
A fallen comrade – one who won't unpack
His kit when he's repatriated back.

Look at these two we pay our taxes for
And work out which does less and which does more;
Then ask, in terms of rates of pay and such,
Why one should get so little, one so much.

The Theatre of War

Time was, the swordsman and the musketeer
Were part of a stage army on parade;
With wooden thrust and firework fusillade
They re-enacted many a brave career;
They fought through all the histories of Shakespeare,
Hardly a duke or earl was left unplayed,
'My kingdom for a horse!' the villain said,
We loved it and could scarce forbear to cheer
Alarms, excursions and the whole charade.
Especially when, at the close of play,
The corpses all got up and walked away.

Today a war can be fought on a fiction,
And has been, yet is the authentic thing,
Waged by elected leaders in our name,
But with a call to arms that lacks conviction;
Their Parliament's a history free zone,
Little is remembered, still less known,
About the human costs of soldiering;
The words are cheap, the blood price is the same,
But still the lofty rhetoric takes wing;
And on this stage of tragedy and sorrow,
The dead won't play the matinee tomorrow.

Agincourt

*'If these men did not die well, it will be a black matter for
the king that led them to it.'*
William Shakespeare, Henry V, Act IV, scene 1.

Remember before Agincourt the thrust
Of Private Williams' royal questioning:
That if the cause of conflict were not just,
It would be a black matter for the king.

So in our time the landscape's dark and bleak
Because the king's successors made it so.
We note that those who know tend not to speak,
And those who speak invariably don't know.

With *X Factor* and *Jungle* escapades,
And *Strictly*'s sequins sparkling in cascades,
And TV personalities in spades,
Disgraced MPs and other renegades,
We've no one but celebrities to throw
Into the breach where heroes used to go.

Challenges and Issues

The great George Orwell got it right: corruption
Is broken language by another name;
And darkness falls without an interruption
Between the word and deed, one and the same;

We cannot even glimpse realities
Through such a cloud of euphemisms and tissues
Of insubstantial words – our tragedies
Arrive disguised as challenges and issues.

When my computer says it has an issue,
It doesn't know the meaning of the noun.
I answer it as Orwell might: 'I wish you
Would just admit you've bloody broken down!'

For every issue there are now solutions;
Which cliché is the worse? The point is moot,
Except to speculate that dissolutions
Are the solutions of the dissolute.

DQF

In March 2011 the BBC, which has a notorious talent for euphemism, announced a cost-cutting exercise under the title 'Delivering Quality First'.

George Orwell would have loved it. Where he worked,
Within the shadows of BBC,
Long after his departure there still lurked
The same aversion to reality.

Against the public interest, quite the worst
Of hatchet jobs in all its history
Was then dressed up in *acronymity*
As DQF: Delivering Quality First.

If in despair, just raise a glass and drink
To the enduring power of doublethink.

Class Warfare

A replay of the politics of class
Is something that I fear may come to pass.
In Parliament, part tragedy part farce,
The cross-party consensus lies in bits,
As shattered as the windows of the Ritz.
So Labour will campaign to be elected
Upon the grievances of the rejected.
The wealthier people and the *jeunesse dorée*
Will be unanimous in voting Tory;
The centre ground's a no man's land – and that's
Not good news for the Liberal Democrats.

Politicians' Call-up

They're partial to the martial metaphor,
But hardly know what the Last Post is for;
The only uniforms they ever wore
Were pinstripes, yet they love the words of war.

The original idea of a campaign
Is military: 'Let's get up and at 'em!'
And naval also, from the Spanish Main
To Scapa Flow and Plymouth Hoe to Chatham.

The opening salvo is the manifesto
To bring opposing forces to a halt.
The election date's announced and then – hey presto!
Their troops are ready for the main assault.

Even the smaller parties can't refrain
From loosing off a policy barrage;
So UKIP's foot-soldiers wage their campaign
Under the orders of General Farage.

The Greens, being peaceful, cannot use bazookas
With which to arm battalion and brigade,
But still they have the firepower of Ms Lucas
To lead their ecological crusade,
And by a *coup de main*, one in a million,
She's now the Member for Brighton Pavilion.

As for the BNP, here let me warn
Nick Griffin's strategy may lie in parking
His tanks upon the other parties' lawn,
And ending up as the MP for Barking.

And so the parties go on operations,
Mail drops and phone banks are their siege machines,
They call their canvassers to battle stations
And politics is war by other means.

Paddy Ashdown

Lord Ashdown of Norton-sub-Hamdon, the former leader of the Liberal Democrats, served in the Royal Marines from 1959 to 1972.

He had all of the leadership ingredients
Just as his Colonel Commandant decreed them:
A knowledge of amphibious machines
And courage short of bellicosity
To be a Captain in the Queen's Marines,
Who followed him not from obedience
They said, but curiosity
To see where he would lead them.

New Labour

The times are sadly out of joint,
We heard the old folk say,
And though they sometimes had a point
They missed the shades of grey:
For governments will disappoint,
But they should not betray.

Coalition (1)

No love was lost 'twixt Liberals and Tories,
One leader called the other one a joke;
Each fired off cannonades of lurid stories
Of campaign promises the other broke.
They battled from Land's End to John O'Groats,
But still they didn't win sufficient votes:
The rising tide just failed to lift their boats.
So then the Tory said to the Lib Dem,
'It's time we tried a different stratagem,
Because of this electoral miscarriage
Let's coalesce and enter into marriage.'
With that the fighting, feuding blues and yellows
Became the very closest of bed-fellows.

(Published in the Eastern Daily Press, *22 May 2010)*

Coalition (2)

Gold-plated David Cameron,
Smooth and urbane, a favoured son,
A privileged and chosen one,
Alumnus of the Bullingdon,
Then had to deal, as leaders ought,
With allies of the rougher sort,
Who questioned the propriety
And value of his Big Society.
And wondered, in the way of a Lib Dem,
What good the Coalition would do them.

Coalition (3)

Nick Clegg, the Deputy Prime Minister, is Liberal Democrat MP for Sheffield (Hallam). Benghazi was the centre of Libyan opposition to Colonel Gaddafi.

The watchword of the times is Coalition,
A ramshackle arrangement, yours and mine,
For bombing Libyan forces to perdition,
Or managing a nation in decline.

In war and peace these closest of allies,
Once mortal foes in parliamentary trenches,
Nod in approval at each other's sallies
Aimed at the dispossessed on Labour's benches.

Yet doubts and dangers stalk the enterprise
And the Lib Dems, whose style is kamikaze,
May hand their enemies a double prize,
The loss of Sheffield (Hallam) and Benghazi.

Cleggmania

On one side stood the hammer and the sickle
And on the other forces of reaction.
But times were hard, allegiances were fickle
And we disliked the politics of faction.

So we triangulated. It seemed brainier
To set the old divisiveness aside.
Two parties wed, the smaller one the bride.
The bliss was brief: Within a year Cleggmania
Had turned to something nearer Cleggicide.

Jerusalem

We've Members we could do without
Who had the nerve to stand again.
We threw some of the villains out,
But others creepily remain.
We made one clean break with the past,
A *Coalition* if you please,
With Clegg in the supporting cast,
And such a mass of new MPs
We hardly can remember them.
We've Cameron and Miliband
On one hand: on the other hand,
The budget cuts are painful and
We've yet to build Jerusalem
In England's green and pleasant land.

The Alternative Vote (1)

*In a referendum on 5 May 2011 the proposal to adopt
a preferential voting system, the Alternative Vote, was defeated
by a margin of more than three to one. I was a Vice Chair of the
'Yes' campaign.*

Our democratic record's rather poor:
Most MPs, lacking popular acclaim,
Are representative only in name;
More people vote against them than vote for.

There was another system in the frame
But, to adopt the racing metaphor,
First past the post, a tired and lame old horse,
Was still the bookies' favourite on a course
Which favoured merit less and habit more.

Alas, our AV had so far to go
To overtake the accursed status quo,
It was the loser in a two-horse race
To win the Democratic Steeplechase.

The Alternative Vote (2)

At first they tried to argue that AV
Would help the extreme right, the BNP.
But then they said the parties would grandstand
To emphasise the centrist and the bland.
But bland extremists? What a contradiction!
Their case imploded as a work of fiction.
Yet sadly that was not the end of it,
For still they won the fateful plebiscite.

The Alternative Vote (3)

Swamping the airwaves with their lies,
The Old Guard and their flacks prevailed;
The democratic option failed,
Torpedoed by mendacities.
The epitaph of our campaign
Was, 'As things have been, things remain'.

Odd People

Kenneth Clarke MP, the Justice Secretary, warned that the introduction of the Alternative Vote could lead to the election of some 'highly odd people'.

It is a measure of our country's health
That it is teeming with the oddest men
And women found in any commonwealth.
Being so wayward, nothing should prevent them
From having odd MPs to represent them.
And since we're talking of eccentrics, Ken,
Could you hark back a bit and tell us when
Were you considered so mainstream yourself?

Rules of War

There was a time, in the Staff College courses,
They taught that men and arms, a zero sum
Assessed as being the balance of two forces,
Would guarantee the battlefield outcome.
Not any more. You'd have to go back years,
To contests of machine guns against spears,
To bombers unopposed and zeppelins,
To great tank battles fought in desert places
And tests of range and blast in battle spaces.
How much less certain is today's warfare
Where force evaporates into thin air,
And front lines are not fixed but anywhere,
A complex, contradictory affair:
The winner loses and the loser wins.

Consider Vietnam, the Tet Offensive:
The Viet Cong's destruction was complete,
The Americans' success was comprehensive,
Yet still they met political defeat.
Public opinion wouldn't bear the cost
When CBS declared the war was lost.
That's the decisive influence of news:
The images of conflict will prevail
And shape the outcomes; force alone will fail.
These are the rules of post-industrial war;
We pay the price and wonder what it's for.
Words are more powerful than shock and awe:
In wars among the people less is more,
And so can losers win and winners lose.

Arab Spring

Events are not free-standing any more,
But cast long shadows over border fences.
Through multiplying webs and blogs and lenses
Autocracies are threatened by the law
Of fierce and unintended consequences.

The old facades of power fall and fold
As tides of protest and revolt rise higher,
Dictators flee and Presidents retire;
Tunisia sneezes, Egypt catches cold,
Damascus smoulders, Bahrain is on fire.

And Libyans in their finest, darkest hour
Rise up amid a multitude of dead,
Killed by a madman, careless as they bled.
His is the ultimate abuse of power,
Who brings the temple down around his head.

With so much revolution in the air,
It seems that no one is untouched by it
Except the cloistered, post-colonial Brit,
Who settles back and has another beer.

Osama Bin Laden

Don't mourn his death but mark it, understood
As owed to those he murdered in cold blood.
Hunted and killed, his body dumped at sea –
Rough justice surely, but not symmetry,
No, not a shadow of equivalence
With his destruction of the innocents.

In Northern Yemen

Weapons of shock and awe fall from the skies
And where they do not kill they traumatise.

Wandering and alone her mother found her,
Just nine years old: the war had raged around her.
In all my life I never saw such eyes,
The haunting, lasting emptiness
Of shell shock, post-traumatic stress,
And wondered, who on earth could be the enemy
Of such a gentle, blameless little Yemeni?

Black Swans

There is a time for peace, a time for war,
A time for rest, a time for being prepared;
You know what I think this is a time for?
It is a time for being really scared.

Nuclear arsenals proliferate,
Pirates and paramilitaries abound,
Calamities of nature devastate,
Once peaceful states become a killing ground.

Jihadists take their own and others' lives,
Cities and suburbs are a firing range,
The culture of blood sacrifice revives;
Darfur is the first war of climate change.

Millions die and still more millions flee
From the great wars of the dark continent;
Others, most desperate, are lost at sea.
The tides are rising and the lives are spent.

Where first the nuclear holocaust began,
An earthquake and near meltdown in Japan
Reveal to us as only Black Swans can
The ultimate destructiveness of man.

Black Swan events are those that cannot hurt us
Because they never have, the world agrees,
Until they do, like fire on phosphorous;
The 9/11 attacks were some of these.

They are the analysts' 'unknown unknowns',
The things we can't predict and never will,
They are not traceable on mapped war zones,
But strike us from the blind side of the hill.

We hear the beating of the Black Swan's wings
Which we thought couldn't happen – we were wrong.
We are beset by strange, outlying things,
And one of these could be the Black Swan's song.

Middle Ground

A quiet life may be a privilege,
But not as much as one at the extremes
Of peace and war and then of love and hate:
The reasonable compromises died,
Illusions don't survive life at the edge,
The middle ground is lost, a field of dreams,
The ceasefires almost all disintegrate,
And opposites attract and then collide.
Caught in the crossfire, we should understand
The middle ground is also no man's land.

Blue Skies

'Cold and timid souls who know neither victory nor defeat.'
Theodore Roosevelt

They guarantee the sun at any price,
The sand and sea and all that other stuff.
I'm unimpressed: the sun's just an old flame,
The brochures oversell the paradise,
The halcyon weather's fine but not enough,
And all blue skies are boringly the same.

I'll take rain in my face, wind in my sails,
The thunder and the lightning heaven-sent;
Give me a storm that's worthy of the name:
A force-ten fury is the prince of gales,
Each gathering of clouds is different,
And all blue skies are boringly the same.

And so with us: there are no starring roles
For those who promenade on Easy Street,
Or bystanders who, to their lasting shame,
Would join the ranks of cold and timid souls
Who know not either victory or defeat.
And all blue skies are boringly the same.

White Christmas

For fifty years we swallowed whole the myth
Of Christmases romanticised by Bing,
Just like the ones we used to know: the whiteness,
The snow and schmaltz and sleigh bells of the dream.

But then we were assailed by the real thing,
Blizzards, black ice and misery therewith;
Such dreadful weather it would strain politeness
To say we were hacked off in the extreme.

The deep mid-winter slid from bad to worse
And hammered us for weeks until we knew
The implications of an ancient curse:
The one that says may all your dreams come true.

Screens

Flat screen or hand held, such a multitude
Of images and messages cascade
In flickering rectangles of light and shade,
Which is the way reality is viewed.

This is no window on the world, my son,
But just a screen in the old-fashioned sense,
An obstacle and electronic fence
Between the eye and what it chances on.

And such a box of tricks, for we will find
In the real world there's no returning whence
We came – and that's the vital difference.
We pass this way but once. There's no rewind.

The Kindle

Do you remember there were books?
At first attracted by their looks,
Then we would open them like lovers
For mysteries within their covers.
We found in them a light divine,
A soul, a spirit and a spine.
They taught us history, art and Greek,
To write, to think, to woo, to speak,
Yet sadly they're in such decline
That they're becoming as antique
As spinning wheel and spindle;
And we're left with the Kindle,
Where people on the Underground
Read slabs unprinted and unbound,
And Paradise will not be found
Nor God's grace shine around.

The Blogosphere

A curse of malediction plagues the net.
It should be a mainstream of our discourse,
But bloggers pour their vitriol through its gutters.
Their ill-intentioned dialogues beget
A wilderness of insult and a force
For mischief on a planet of the nutters.

There are two rival theories to explain
Such incoherent incivilities:
Either they're due to drugs and alcohol,
Or else the fingers far outpace the brain;
While digits furiously pound they keys,
The faculty of reason's gone AWOL.

Illusion

This is included in honour of my grandfather Robert Bell, former news editor of the London Observer. *It comes from his book of poems* After-thoughts, *published in 1929 by Methuen, who described them as touching 'with feeling and fancy upon life'.*

The white house glimmers through the trees:
The grave and gentle candles shine.
'Here, surely, here at last is peace' …
Perhaps he thinks the same of mine.

Lines

Adrian Bell, Robert Bell's son and my father, was a lifelong, unwavering and supercharged romantic. His lines 'on seeing a pair of porcelain figures overshadowed by a red rose' were included in his Poems, *published by Cobden-Sanderson in 1935.*

He leans to thee with fragile courtesy,
His eyes star-brightened by Love's breathing wing:
O tip-toe trance of soft encountering!
Thy shady bower
Of many-petalled flower,
Which, Nature's fantasy, is full as fair as thou;
But even now
It droops with prescience of mortality.

When Troubles Come

I booked a train, but then a cursed fault,
A signal failure outside Bletchley station,
Brought every Euston service to a halt
Across the board – a total cancellation.

And so instead I drove my ancient Rover
On what became a motorway too far;
A broken clutch announced the journey over,
And desperate, I hired another car.

Then, where the road and rail ran parallel,
I saw from my expensive limousine
The trains were thundering past and going well,
While I was in the traffic jam from hell.
I sat awhile amid this dismal scene,
In contemplation of what might have been
And in distrust of every wheeled machine.

Shakespeare was right and prescient and wise:
When troubles come they come not single spies.

TGV

President Pompidou once chided his countrymen for their ill humour – 'la morosité française'.

I'm suffering from visitor's *tristesse*,
Because the French appear to have a need
To travel in high dudgeon at high speed;
And since I would prefer a gentler pace,
I tend to find the *Train à Grande Vitesse*
Is not so much a journey as a race
Run by them all with great *morosité*,
Competing and complaining all the way.
So from the Gare de Lyon to Marseille
I'll take the stopping service, if I may.

Anagrams

A man of words drew on his wide experience
Of texts and transcripts over many years,
To note the irony that Presbyterians
Is letter-wise the same as Britney Spears.

Our wordsmith, waxing spiritual again,
Was able likewise to reverse the polar
Opposites of sacred and profane:
He turned Episcopal to Pepsi-Cola.

But what did for him was a metaphor
For tyranny both functional and titular,
When he unwisely said that Mother-in-law
Was virtually the same as Woman Hitler.

Tory Dictionary

Satisfactory
Is a True Blue who likes things as they are,
Conservatory
Is one who strives to keep them up to par,
Inflammatory
Is one whose rhetoric has gone too far,
Desultory
But, lacking staying power and stamina,
Transitory
Has vanished from the scene, a shooting star.
Territory
Is where a Tory comes upon new ground,
Ambulatory
And reconnoitres it, by walking round,
Inventory
Then makes a list of everything he's found
Nugatory
And throws it out, deciding it's unsound.
Offertory
Is a Conservative with ample coffers,
Predatory
Is one who grabs what life's unfairness offers,
Congratulatory
Is for all those whom self-doubt never bothers,
Derogatory
The most nay-saying and ill-natured of us.
Accusatory
Is one whose common charity is nowhere,

Amatory
Is far too loving for a Tory – whoa there!
Suppository
The best advice is, let's not even go there.

Kurt Schork

Kurt Schork, the Reuters reporter in Sarajevo from 1992 to 1995,
was killed in Sierra Leone in 2000.

They turn up in their combats, clean and pressed,
Equipped with body armour, suave and willing
To go to war even in the cannon's mouth.
But then it starts and they are unimpressed,
They'd rather keep their distance from the killing.
The war is to the north and they head south.

There's something to the risk of being killed
That tends to put the *fashionista* off;
He looks the part over a war zone beer,
In showmanship he is uniquely skilled,
But face to face with a Kalashnikov
He likes to change his mind and go elsewhere.

But there's another who won't talk so much;
Scruffy and unkempt he quietly loiters
Unrecognised and, cut down in his prime,
Has done the business honestly. One such:
The unsurpassable Kurt Schork of Reuters,
One of the heroes of my life and time.

From Sarajevo to Afghanistan
He was the guiding light and exemplar,
Conscience in residence of the press corps,
A good reporter and still better man,
Until the day he took a risk too far
And perished in a futile foreign war.

Reporters' Retreat

We noticed they were booted and were spurred
In case the wars that they dreamed of occurred.
They looked the part and talked it more or less,
Flak jacketed and ready for combat.
They were impressive in their fluency,
But offered little more than style and dress.
The truth is they were not where it was at,
Their war reporting was a kind of truancy;
They worked within the green zones and without
Apparently the will to venture out;
Their offices were underground – and that
Hardly proclaimed the heroism of the press.

Censorship

The television networks are programmed
With guidelines that restrict and curbs that chafe;
They've given up on 'Publish and be damned',
And substituted 'Censor and be safe'.

Their managements don't see war as it is,
But rather as a breach of etiquette;
Opinion polls are paramount in this:
The viewers wouldn't wish to be upset.

And if we field men ever sought to show
The truth about a war, or something like it,
The upper floor invariably said no:
The editors would shake their heads and spike it.

In zones of war and conflict where the press
Are sent to make some kind of reckoning,
We falsified – I literally confess
I never really showed a bloody thing.

So Ministers of the Crown who never
Perceived the truth, because the truth was hid,
Saw warfare as a glorious endeavour:
'Let's go for it,' they said – and so they did.

Tim Hetherington

Tim Hetherington, British photographer and film-maker,
was killed in Libya in April 2011.

We spend our lives in trivial pursuits
And little kingdoms much like King Canute's.
Even our causes are so close to home
They frankly don't amount to all that much:
The right to demonstrate, the right to strike,
The right to privacy, the right to roam,
Flight paths, foot paths, wind farms and the like:
These are the so-and-so, the such-and-such.

But there's another harder, darker side
About which we know the square root of damn all,
A world of forced migrations, genocide,
The suicide of Mladic's own daughter,
Of wars for scarce resources, oil and water,
Of jihadists with children in their thrall,
And continental and industrial slaughter.

This was the world, extreme and actual,
In which he lived as witness and reporter
Bearing the torch of truth, only to fall
The victim of a random Libyan mortar.

The Death of News

'The only qualities essential for real success in journalism are rat-like cunning, a plausible manner and a little literary ability'
Nicholas Tomalin of the Sunday Times

News-chasing then, we'd hit the airport running,
Often in just the clothes that we stood up in,
With everything to gain, nothing to lose;
A way with words and certain rat-like cunning
Was all it took, said our Nick Tomalin,
And what we did looked, read and felt like news.

But though the new technology abounded,
The adventure ended, swiftly and discreetly,
On someone's orders, none of us knew whose;
The death knell for real journalism sounded,
When health and safety did for it completely:
It died and was replaced by pseudo-news.

Acts of self-harm and sabotage took place
As readerships declined and staffs down-scaled.
Abandoning inherited values,
Managements went on a wild paper chase
To find a new agenda – and they failed.
Whatever else it was, it wasn't news.

How shamelessly they harvested this stuff;
Remember Holly, Jessica and Madeleine?
The media army camped at Praia da Luz,
For whom any old rumour was enough,
Exploiting private grief for corporate gain?
A fitting term for it was necro-news.

These days they don't report, they just perform,
Waving their arms in fake sincerity;
Hardly a gimmick that they won't refuse:
Lip gloss for men is actually the norm.
What's missing is the authenticity,
The being there which is the heart of news.

They'll prance and strut before a video wall,
Or cower within the Green Zone in Iraq,
'Twixt frying pan and fire it's hard to choose,
The circus masters have them in their thrall.
We know full well that there's no going back,
And that is why we mourn the death of news.

(Published in the British Journalism Review, *March 2010)*

Neutrality

'I'll be a candle-holder and look on'
Romeo in Shakespeare's Romeo and Juliet, *Act I, scene 4*

A feckless pastor in the Sunshine State
Summons the press, sets fire to the Koran;
With images of hatred in full spate,
His bonfire, being broadcast, seals the fate
Of blameless victims in Afghanistan.

Time was, we tried to balance the equation,
We weighed the pros and cons, not very well,
Being even-handed between Heaven and Hell;
Then closed the piece with an absurd evasion:
'One thing is certain, only time will tell.'

'I'll be a candle-holder and look on.'
Oh no, you won't. The fierce phenomenon
Of rolling news means those days are long gone.
You can't claim to be neutral any more
When you're complicit in a Holy War.

Bad News

I've seen it on the news and so it's true,
The camera of course will tell no lies;
Dear trusting friend and dupe, if you but knew
What I have learned, you might think otherwise.

The sort of people whom the trade attracts
Are those who think that they can best succeed
At the expense of others, and don't need
To pay too much attention to the facts.

I'd say, look carefully before crediting
The authenticity of what you see;
A multitude of sins lies in the editing.
Beware the unholy trinity
Of I, myself and me.

I know a man of dubious honesty
Whose practice was to stage some brave foray
Shot in a peaceful suburb of Grozny:
The actual war was several miles away.

Another vain and self-regarding type
Enhanced an ever-growing reputation
With front-line exploits magnified by hype
And stories which were marvels of inflation;
His tales of people that he knew
And instances of derring-do
Were largely fabrication.

It is an issue worth attending to,
The incidence of electronic sleaze.
The scoundrels may be relatively few:
We used to think the same of our MPs.

Strictly

When I set out it was a simpler time:
We thought we had a mission to inform,
But then show business changed the paradigm;
The new imperative is to perform,
And puppet shows are going down a storm.

These days it's not enough to stand and state,
The old composure has been shown the door.
The modern way is to gesticulate,
They've no idea what human speech is for,
And journalism's a branch of semaphore.

I'd like to think that in the present rage
Of showmanship the truth is still a factor.
Probably not – for all the world's a stage,
And the reporter on it is an actor,
His ego like a nuclear reactor.

Where will this end? Sometimes it seems to me,
If news continues down this road, consorting
With all the nonsense of celebrity,
The tinsel trappings and red carpetry,
It will turn into *Strictly Come Reporting*.

More or Less

The golden rule for those reporting war
Is not to be enamoured of the violence;
They have to understand that less is more.
The hardest art is that of writing silence.

The whisper's more effective than the shout,
And many words say much less than a few.
When I was asked, 'What's your report about?'
I'd say, 'About a minute forty two.'

Golden Age

For all those years the business worked just fine:
Our film was shot and parcelled and air-freighted;
The old technology left us alone
To do much as we wished in the front line,
The health and safety guidelines were all mine;
Our speed perhaps was somewhat porcupine,
But our reports were eagerly awaited.
The good times ended when the mobile phone
Arrived unheralded in the war zone.
Next thing we knew (the interval was fleeting)
We stopped reporting and we started tweeting.

Haiti

The poorest country in the hemisphere
Is devastated by its largest quake.
You think the aircraft engines that you hear
Mean help is coming? That is your mistake.

More than a million with their needs unmet
Are crying out in unrelieved distress;
The only fresh supplies they seem to get
Are the unwanted convoys of the press.

Legions of hacks are drawn into this trouble,
And settling on it, much like flies on shit,
Their microphones eavesdropping in the rubble,
The worse it gets, the more they relish it.

The press of course are watered and they're fed;
And leaving their humanity behind,
They'll venture out to walk among the dead
And close their hearts to most of what they find.

Of course they show concern and sympathy;
Compassion is part of their stock in trade.
They will impress with their sincerity,
And if they can fake that, they've got it made.

In such a scene a journalist at large
Once wrote a script that was a pack of lies;
The judges called it vivid reportage,
And then awarded him their highest prize.

With media reputations to be made,
Some would prefer the rescuers to fail;
Bad news is a commodity for sale,
And journalism is the cruellest trade.

Babylon

Across the Caribbean Sea
The steel bands lack variety,
Playing the same tunes endlessly:
Just *Yellow Bird* and *Island in the Sun*.
Yet there's another, deeper, scriptural one
To keep an inner and eternal eye on,
The pulsing legend of an age long gone:
By the rivers of Babylon
Yea we wept when we sat down
And we remembered Zion.

And we in our time need to be draconian,
Because our own predicament,
So far from being heaven-sent
Looks downright Babylonian.

Suffolk

Dunwich beneath the sea; a castle wall
Built of the flint and stones of Framlingham;
The village graveyards' *In Memoriam*;
The timbered majesty of Lavenham,
The graceful Swan, the firing of the bells;
The Bull, the White Horse, Angel and Dun Cow;
The Regimental quick march 'Speed the Plough';
The landscapes in which Constable excels;
The market towns without a shopping mall;
The essence of high Suffolk, Redisham;
The vaulted tracery of Elveden Hall;
The fabled sciapod of Dennington,
Which used its foot to shield it from the sun;
The church at Blythburgh, mystical and lonely;
The sign that reads 'To Barsham City only';
The amber of Covehithe and the sea shells;
The ghosts of aircraft haunting Stradishall;
From Newmarket to Walberswick to Eye,
The oldest fields beneath the widest sky,
And still the greatest glory of it all
Is that it's on the way to nowhere else.

Windfall

'I am a lawyer from Burkina Faso;
Following a raid by pirates off Bossaso,
My client, a tribal Chief sadly deceased,
Died wishing that your wealth should be increased.
His next of kin lost in the tragedy
Leave you, Dear Sir, his only legatee.
I also have to tell you his largesse
Is seven million dollars worth, no less.
I need the details of your bank account,
And you will then receive the full amount.'

Isn't it touching that the dear departed
Of Africa can be so open-hearted?
Or is it possible that piracy
Does not occur exclusively at sea?

Absurdistan

Ingenious nations have devised a plan
To make a profit from their fighting men:
They park them somewhere in Absurdistan,
And all the bills are paid by the UN.

These are peacekeepers with so light a touch,
They play their video games and volleyball
Behind the wire and, soldiering not much,
They might as well not be deployed at all.

But they will bear the guilt if, nothing worth
And looking only to their own defence,
This land, one of the poorest on the earth,
Dies a slow death at the UN's expense.

Congo

Joseph Conrad's Heart of Darkness *was based on his experience as a riverboat captain on the Congo River in 1890. Roger Casement, later executed for treason, was the British Consul in the Congo Free State at the time.*

Heart of Darkness was his masterpiece;
He lived it and he wrote it from the Congo,
About the conquests of King Leopold
And inhumanity of men to men.
But times change: those were those and these are these;
Under the shadow of Mount Nyiragongo,
More lives are being traded for fool's gold:
The Congo's even darker now than then.

In this the Great War of the continent,
A stain of blood on Africa's great lakes,
Four million lost their lives in a decade;
Again, these times are these and those were those.
There is no witness, Conrad or Casement,
No one whose testimony awakes
And stirs the conscience for a new crusade:
The difference now is that nobody knows.

Or cares – these are hard times for a crusader;
The news is only where reporters are,
The Congo is too distant and remote,
The press have lost the nerve to operate,
The darkness doesn't show on their radar,
They see it as a no man's land too far;
Its turmoil will not move a single vote
In the short term – but long term, just you wait!

Datelines

It was the dateline that defined the antics
Of us old hacks, incurable romantics:
A sort of verbal picture frame or prism
To introduce our kind of journalism.
Filing from Africa became a race
To find the most outlandish time and place:
The winner was the man who opened one day
With the immortal line, 'Banana, Sunday'.

Dubai

Where once a trading post slept in the sand,
Fantastic edifices scrape the sky;
Forget the golden road to Samarkand,
Behold the glittering city of Dubai
In which Arabia meets Disneyland.

A ski slope in a desert shopping mall –
Such breath-taking excesses come to pass,
That the sheer ostentation of it all
May signify the pride before the fall,
As in the time of Ozymandias.

There's alcohol inside the crystal glass,
And girls from Kazakhstan patrol the bars;
And yet the jihadists have passed it by,
This shining soaring city of Dubai,
As if it isn't there. I wonder why.

Iceland

The Arctic island functions like a freezer,
But also pulses with infernal forces,
The hot spring, the volcano and the geyser:
But none of these are bankable resources.

This was the natural deficit that led it
To trade casino-style in easy credit;
And foreign trust funds spiralled into debt
By risking all on Reykjavik roulette.

You'd think that such a place would not be harmful,
But you'd be wrong. The system failed because it
Printed off paper assets by the armful
And Mr Gullible lost his deposit.

And there was worse, for following the panic,
The savings meltdown and the market crash,
The flow of credit and the ebb of cash,
The Icelandic fury then became volcanic
And covered all of Europe in its ash.

St Helena

The Saints are the island's inhabitants.

The world's remotest island – cliffs of granite,
The fortress where a dream of empire died,
Is changeless since the time of Bonaparte.
It is the biggest pebble on the planet,
Defended by the ocean either side,
The island jail that broke his stubborn heart.

We fail our history if we idealise:
Death stalked this rock. The churchyard holds the graves
Of British officers who died at sea.
More of a prison than a paradise,
It was the home to slave masters and slaves,
The final colony to set them free.

The world's first concentration camp was here,
Established by the British for the Boers.
Then it was violent and now it's bust.
The younger Saints seek lives and jobs elsewhere,
There's nothing for them on these barren shores,
Only the relics of colonial wars
And ghosts of admirals and emperors.
Britannia rules these waves – but only just.

Suez and Panama

The two canals' biography
Is something of a mystery:
One's changing its geography,
The other one its history.

In Panama the aim's to maximise
And virtually rebuild the whole canal;
With new locks of a super-tanker size
And super transit fees the matching prize,
It is the world's earth-moving capital.

Suez by contrast likes to let things be
And just rework the past for all it's worth;
Erecting monuments to victory
In battles that were lost in '73
Is easier by far than moving earth.

Border Lines

The Sykes–Picot agreement, reached secretly in 1916 between British and French diplomats, established the present-day borders of Iraq.

A rule of war is that straight lines on maps
Are auguries of subsequent mishaps,
And those who drew them, such as Sykes–Picot,
Were architects of an imbroglio;
For boundaries were not so neat by chance,
But ill-bequeathed by Britain and by France.
Geometry is not in nature's order
And geography will make a better border.
Mountains, rift valleys and remotest shores
Are nature's own impediments to wars;
So countries with the wildest fluctuations
Of border lines are the most favoured nations.

Baseball

They found a game remarkably like cricket
Without the fine leg, cover drive or wicket,
And turned it somehow (there are many theories)
Into a strange and alien sport, of medium
Complexity and unremitting tedium,
Played by Americans and Japanese,
Canadians and Cubans, none but these,
And called it the World Series.

The Banker

I have no prejudice or rancour
Against the profiteering banker;
But if he reckons that the onus
Should fall on us to pay his bonus,
Then I'm the Maharajah of Sri Lanka.

Tax Demand

Our hard-faced rulers urge that we should fund them
By paying extra taxes to the Crown.
We answer *Nil illegitimi carborundum*,
Don't ever let the bastards grind you down!

Ballade of Old Age

Declining years? So be it. We'll decline
The fashions and the fads that irritate,
The excess of midriff and the lack of spine,
The Twitter and the Facebook in full spate.
'You don't win games with kids.' Hard to relate,
It takes a while to turn boys into men
And put the potent into potentate,
For life begins at three score years and ten.

In what they call their music they combine
Demented drums and discords to create
A racket like the curse of Frankenstein
Whose only purpose is to aggravate
And give us something righteously to hate.
They are but cuckoo clocks to our Big Ben,
We'll see them off before we lie in state,
For life begins at three score years and ten.

Their love life is completely out of line,
Their ladies are absurdly underweight,
The merest wisps of things, too anodyne
For men of substance to appreciate.
Our years are reasons to accelerate
And not to settle for the long amen;
Myself, I plan to stay up rather late,
For life begins at three score years and ten.

Envoi
Your Majesty, Elizabeth the Great,
Our Monarch since we can't remember when,
Your heir apparent's going to have to wait,
For life begins at three score years and ten.

Royal Wedding (1)

Prince William and Kate Middleton were married in
Westminster Abbey on 29 May 2011.

The valleys celebrate and hills
Rejoice because of Kate and Wills.
The headline writers palpitate
At the approach of Wills and Kate.
Only the gloomy *Guardian*, in despair,
Wishes the Royal Couple were elsewhere.

Royal Wedding (2)

Republicans have all the arguments:
Why should the Royal Family be succeeding
In either sense by accident of birth?
The case seems so clear-cut for Presidents
Chosen by ballot rather than by breeding,
So we – not they – may inherit the earth,

But ultimately, when push comes to shove,
As with the million in the Park and Mall
When William and his Catherine tied the knot,
What's left without the loyalty and love,
The Crown and grand tradition of it all?
We're really better served by what we've got.

Retrospective

I saw myself from forty years ago
As someone whom I wouldn't wish to know.
This young reporter I was looking at,
I didn't like his morals or his hat,
His escapades, his dubious love affairs,
His haircut or his loafers or his flares,
The accent of his broadcasts, so cut-glass
In imitation of the ruling class;
But most of all the insolence of youth,
As if he, and he only, knew the truth.

He for his part would not accept the blame
For what his later character became,
Transformed from a Young Turk to an old codger,
From bright young thing to veteran bomb-dodger.

There is one point on which we both agree,
Although we share the same identity:
This other fellow really can't be me!

The Celebrity Protection Force

I scanned the news from Camden Town to Morden:
Celebrities competed with each other,
Not politicians, David against Gordon,
But refugees from *Strictly* and *Big Brother*.

It's surely long past time we threw a cordon
Around this stuff, declared an armistice.
It's gone too far: the country known as Jordan
Is now a synonym for Katie Price.

Although she's not at war with all and sundry,
This tabloid icon is at action stations;
Her enemy is her ex, one Peter Andre.
Who says we don't need the United Nations?

Let's form a force to monitor their actions,
Give it blue helmets, armoured cars and more,
To halt the famous-for-five-minutes factions:
And find a name for it – CELEBPROFOR.

Cheryl

I see the nation is entranced by Cheryl
And ask, is she a singer or an actress?
A princess, patron saint or benefactress?
A businesswoman, owning many factories?
An editor perhaps or a redactress?
And am I ignorant of her at my peril?

Max

When he was only four my grandson Max,
Whose escapades gave rise to heart attacks,
Struck his first match: and as the flames rose higher
My little cottage was engulfed by fire.

Now more than twelve, I'm sure that Maximilian,
A piece of work and one kid in a million,
Will make his mark upon the larger stage.
And, even more than his beloved mother,
Will have his name all over the front page,
Sooner or later, one way or another.

Decisions

We tend to cringe so much and self-berate
Whenever we commit the Great Mistake,
That it should help to set the record straight,
And list the missteps that we didn't make.

Let this be known, across a chequered life,
And weighing one deliverance with another:
I neither danced for *Strictly*'s Bruce Forsyth,
Nor signed an unwise contract with *Big Brother*.
But once, beguiled by the presenter's wink,
I did agree to play *The Weakest Link*.

Radio Five Live

It started out in warfare and mayhem
And in those days was known as Scud FM;
But had appeal
Perceived and real
To regular and ordinary folk,
So now it's better known as Radio Bloke.

Classic FM

If I were to be Supreme Ruler, the first act of my dictatorship
would be to revoke the broadcasting licence of Classic FM. Simon
Bates no longer works for the station, but the memory lingers on.

Though some of what they play is quite sublime,
The engulfing chatter is more than enough
To ruin it when almost every time
They back announce the music as 'great stuff'.

Thus *La Bohème* is great stuff by Puccini,
They flog great stuff by Holst and Liszt to death,
Great stuff by Chopin, Brahms and Paganini,
Great stuff by everyone across the board,
Vivaldi's *Seasons*, Sullivan's *Lost Chord*,
Come into the Garden – great stuff! – *Maud*;
And then, illiterate, they pause for breath
Between Arturo – gulp! – and Toscanini.

So when the DJ Simon Bates
Turns up outside the Pearly Gates
And clamours for inclusion,
St Peter would do really well,
In choosing between Heaven and Hell,
To test his elocution.

Mother Tongue

The Bible (King James version) and Shakespeare
Are to our tongue what Machiavelli's Prince
Was to the politics of courtly Florence.
Alas, the language went downhill from there,
And what has happened to it since
Is cause for much abhorrence.

Language

Somewhere between Exeter and Reading
I travelled in astonishment awhile:
A fellow passenger produced a file
Some forty pages thick, under the heading
Brand and Generic Keyword Optimisation.
Was this the language Shakespeare wrote,
Or something coded and remote,
A symphony without a note,
Defying explanation?

Word Abuse

With clichés scattered over a wide area,
And moving forward, at this point in time,
Through sea change, step change and a paradigm,
For rolling out a fit-for-purpose plan
(Whoever rolled one *in*, you witless man?),
Because it's as contagious as malaria,
This word abuse deserves a total ban.

Painted Lady

I met a girl on one of Cunard's ships
Who had the whole world at her finger tips;
The thought occurred, wherever this one sails,
She's going to be as colourful as nails.
Ranges of peacock colours were displayed
In varnishes of every hue and shade.
So naturally in the Caribbean
She opted for a deep aquamarine;
Off the Pacific coast of Mexico
She changed to sparkling grey and indigo.
She will of course use matching paints that please
While sailing in the Red and Yellow Seas,
And in the Coral Sea it's only moral
To use a tint respectful of the coral;
But when we reach the coast of Eritrea,
If pirate ships should threaten to waylay her,
Then that will be my signal to take charge
And paint her nails throughout in camouflage.

The Virtues

The first girl whom I met was Charity
Who told me with quite brutal clarity
That I required a total overhaul.
The next in line I met another, Constance,
Who notwithstanding my remonstrance
Turned out to have no constancy at all.
I tried a Patience and she mine: ere long
She proved to be impossibly headstrong.
I met a Faith and found beyond dispute
Fidelity was not her strongest suit.
I thought that Prudence could have had potential,
Except that she was not at all prudential.
My Verity was fraudulent and ruthless
And, sad to say, exceptionally truthless.
And lastly there was Hope, but everywhere
All those who knew her also knew despair.
I have forgotten or lost in obscurity
Whether I ever knew a girl called Purity.

War Wounds

*In August 1992 in Sarajevo I was expertly treated for a mortar
wound at the United Nations Field Hospital, run by the
French. On leaving the hospital I found that all my money
had disappeared.*

Once in a war I took a double hit,
Shelled by the Serbs and plundered by the French
(Each side, you might say, playing to its strength),
But I recovered and got over it.

Years later, I was mortared in the heart
By one who didn't wish to make me suffer,
But left me melancholy and apart,
And getting over that was so much tougher.

Trajectories

True love begins where their affections merge,
(To seek its wilder shores would just be silly),
And ends where their trajectories diverge:
His is the Northern, hers the Piccadilly.
And thus the escalator at King's Cross
Becomes a moving metaphor of loss.

End Game

You brought me joy and grief, you fickle female,
And when I'm gone, if you still misbehave,
You can expect to get a scorching email
From somewhere on the far side of the grave.

The Toast Rack

I have a friend who keeps an old toast rack
Upon her desk in which to file her post;
As a result she rather tends to lack
A place in which to put her morning toast.

Museum Piece

The exhibition 'War Reporting: The War Correspondent Under Fire Since 1914' opened at the Imperial War Museum North in May 2011.

I filled in loan agreements by the yard,
They asked for souvenirs lest they forget,
I lent them an accreditation card,
A white suit, dog tags and an epaulette.
They then complained the card was stained with mould;
What else did they expect from one so old?

So many years have passed since I set forth,
Ambition dwindles and the life force with it:
And at the last I'm merely an exhibit
In the Imperial War Museum North.

Credo

Because timidity invites disgrace,
Don't ever hesitate to show your face,
However dark and dangerous the place:
You make a difference or you fill a space.

Where you have principles do not forsake them,
Where you have fears and frailties forget them:
Good things happen because people make them,
And bad things happen because people let them.

Point of Departure

Three score and ten, I'm feeling mortal,
Reviewing times unprofitably spent,
Little to celebrate, lots to repent;
The years successively accelerate,
The candle gutters and the hour is late.
With boarding pass in hand at life's last portal,
There's no mistaking the departure gate;
I wonder, as I rise to take my leave,
What did I ever actually achieve?

Epitaph

When I am gone, I hope you'll pause a minute
And say, sadly not to my face,
The world's a slightly less worse place
Because of my time in it.
But, just as probably, you may recall
I made no bloody difference at all.

Index of first lines

Heart of Darkness was his masterpiece; 124
He had all of the leadership ingredients 78
He leans to thee with fragile courtesy, 100
He made his reputation in committee; 53
Here was a man who lived not by the sword 28
He sat before me in a guarded cell, 26
He seemed a decent sort, upright and staid, 40
He was installed Chief of the General Staff 54
He wrote his operas to great acclaim, 35

'I am a lawyer from Burkina Faso; 122
Ian Duncan Smith 48
I booked a train, but then a cursed fault, 101
I drove at speed across the airport runway, 23
I filled in loan agreements by the yard, 151
If you should wonder why we breathed our last, 9
I have a friend who keeps an old toast rack 150
I have no prejudice or rancour 132
I met a girl on one of Cunard's ships 145
I'm suffering from visitor's tristesse, 102
Indifferent to the people's warning, 39
In discharge of their parliamentary duties, 44
In fifty years I never played the hero 18
Ingenious nations have devised a plan 123
In the tradition of the music hall 10
Iraq, Afghanistan, now Libya too, 4
I saw myself from forty years ago 136
I scanned the news from Camden Town to Morden: 137
I see the nation is entranced by Cheryl 138
It almost seemed an age of innocence 41
It had the aspect of a high romance, 21
It is a measure of our country's health 86
It is to me a cause of deepest regret 32
It started out in warfare and mayhem 141
It was the dateline that defined the antics 125
It was the ultimate war zone hotel, 24
I've seen it on the news and so it's true, 113
I wish I had my own duck house, 42

News-chasing then, we'd hit the airport running, 110
No love was lost 'twixt Liberals and Tories, 80
No need to whip the poor backbencher 38

Once in a war I took a double hit, 147
One day beneath a tree in Costa Rica 32
One day in autumn 1964, 15
One night in Tottenham we crossed a border 1
On one side stood the hammer and the sickle 82
Our democratic record's rather poor: 84
Our hard-faced rulers urge that we should fund them 132

'Please take a seat, Prime Minister, and stay, 7
Prime Minister Anthony Lynton Blair 49

Remember before Agincourt the thrust 72
Republicans have all the arguments: 135

Satisfactory 104
Since seagulls are so common everywhere, 32
Somewhere between Exeter and Reading 143
Somewhere remote and safe, out in the sticks, 47
Swamping the airwaves with their lies, 85

The Americans, sensing trouble up ahead, 69
The Arctic island functions like a freezer, 127
The Bible (King James version) and Shakespeare 143
The Big Man called his people to the square, 17
The cat looked up at the bird in its nest, 33
The claim was clear, without a caveat, 51
The danger level was high and rising higher, 31
The doomed 18th Division went to war 59
The first girl whom I met was Charity 146
The first of life's inspections that I failed 12
The flag-draped coffins now exceed twelve score 57
The flags were lowered, one by one, 19
The Generals of my youth were bright and zestful, 68
The golden rule for those reporting war 116

We knew his scowl, his cold contempt, his swagger, 27
We noticed they were booted and were spurred 107
We sold them armaments and armoured cars, 16
We spend our lives in trivial pursuits 109
We tend to cringe so much and self-berate 140
We've Members we could do without 83
'What lessons should I learn if my ambition 67
When first I walked in past the grand statues, 37
When he was only four my grandson Max, 139
When I am gone, I hope you'll pause a minute 154
When I served in the ranks the then CO 14
When I set out it was a simpler time: 115
Where once a trading post slept in the sand, 126
With clichés scattered over a wide area, 144

You brought me joy and grief, you fickle female, 149

Index of titles